Also by Virginia A. Tashjian

ONCE THERE WAS AND WAS NOT

Illustrated by Nonny Hogrogian

Juba This
and
Juba That

Juba This
and
Juba That

Story Hour Stretches for Large or Small Groups

Selected by
VIRGINIA A. TASHJIAN

with Illustrations by
Victoria de Larrea

Boston   Little, Brown and Company   Toronto

Acknowledgments for material in this book may be
found on page 114

*Published simultaneously in Canada
by Little, Brown & Company (Canada) Limited*

PRINTED IN THE UNITED STATES OF AMERICA

For My Favorite Storyteller—
My Mother, Zvart Agababian

CONTENTS

TO BOYS AND GIRLS

This book contains chants, poetry, stories, finger plays, riddles, songs, tongue twisters and jokes that are fun to sing, tell, and play.

Try them at home or at school, in your scout, church or club meetings, or anywhere that friends gather together. Perhaps you will enjoy them so much that you will want to make up some of your own.

Juba This
and
Juba That

CHANTS

Chants are a very old form of group entertainment. Here are five. Follow the leader's actions carefully, be very dramatic and you will have fun playing them over and over again.

Juba

Juba this and Juba that
Juba killed a yellow cat
Juba up and Juba down
Juba runnin' all around.

The leader first recites the verse and the group repeats it several times. The actions are added one at a time:

FIRST TIME: *repeat verse slowly and very loudly in singsong cadence.*

SECOND TIME: *repeat verse a little faster and a little more softly in a singsong cadence. At the same time clap hands in rhythm.*

THIRD TIME: *repeat verse a little faster and even more softly. Slap both hands on knees and then clap hands together in rhythm.*

FOURTH TIME: *repeat verse very fast in a very soft voice. At the same time, slap hands on knees, clap hands together, clap hands to both cheeks, clap hands together again in rhythm.*

The leader may repeat the chant as many times as the group wishes, making up more actions.

Head and Shoulders, Baby

*Players touch both hands to head and shoulders and clap on
"one, two three." Other actions are done as suggested in verse.
Still others may be added as desired.*

Head and shoulders, Baby—one, two, three.
Head and shoulders, Baby—one, two, three.
Head and shoulders, head and shoulders,
Head and shoulders, Baby—one, two, three.

Knee and ankle, Baby—one, two, three.
Knee and ankle, Baby—one, two, three.
Knee and ankle, knee and ankle,
Knee and ankle, Baby—one, two, three.

Touch the ground, Baby—one, two, three.
Touch the ground, Baby—one, two, three.
Touch the ground, touch the ground,
Touch the ground, Baby—one, two, three.

Stand up, sit down, Baby—one, two, three.
Stand up, sit down, Baby—one, two, three.
Stand up, sit down, stand up, sit down,
Stand up, sit down, Baby—one, two, three.

Who Did?

All clap in rhythm as the leader chants the call in a singsong cadence and the children repeat the response.

CALL: Who did?
RESPONSE: *Who did?*
CALL: Who did?
RESPONSE: *Who did?*
ALL: Who did swallow Jo-Jo-Jo-Jo?

Who did?
  Who did?
Who did?
  Who did?
ALL: Who did swallow Jo-Jo-Jo-Jo?

Who did?
  Who did?
Who did?
  Who did?
Who did swallow Jonah?
  Who did swallow Jonah?
ALL: Who did swallow Jonah down?

Whale did.
  Whale did.
Whale did.
  Whale did.
ALL: Whale did swallow Jo-Jo-Jo-Jo.

Whale did.
  Whale did.
Whale did swallow Jonah.
  Whale did swallow Jonah.
ALL: Whale did swallow Jonah up.

Gabriel.
  Gabriel.
Gabriel.
  Gabriel.
ALL: Gabriel, blow your trump-trump-trump-trump.

Gabriel.
  Gabriel.
Gabriel.
  Gabriel.
ALL: Gabriel, blow your trumpet loud!

Old Hogan's Goat

Although this may be sung, it is also effective as a chant. The leader chants each line, which is repeated exactly by the children. All clap hands and tap feet in rhythm to the chanting.

Old Hogan's goat
Was feelin' fine,
He ate a red shirt
Right off the line.

I took a stick
And beat his back,
And tied him to
A railroad track.

A speeding train
Was adrawin' nigh,
Old Hogan's goat
Was doomed to die.

He gave an aw-
ful shriek of pain,
Coughed up that shirt
And flagged that train.

The Dark House

The leader chants each line or every half-line in a soft, slow, sepulchral voice. Children repeat each line in the same way. The telling becomes more ghostly and spooky with each line. The last word is a sudden shout!

In a dark, dark wood, there was a dark, dark house,
And in that dark, dark house, there was a dark, dark room,
And in that dark, dark room, there was a dark, dark cupboard,
And in that dark, dark cupboard, there was a dark, dark shelf,
And in that dark, dark shelf, there was a dark, dark box,
And in that dark, dark box, there was a GHOST!

POETRY AND RHYME

Read these poems at different speeds, finishing the rhymes and guessing the subject of some of them. Then make up some limericks of your own to share with your group.

Seven Little Rabbits

As the leader begins to read this, the repetition will be obvious, and the children will chime in. The leader must begin speaking very slowly so that she can go faster and faster and have enough breath left to finish very fast indeed.

Seven little rabbits
Walkin' down the road
Walkin' down the road
Seven little rabbits
Walkin' down the road
To call on old friend toad.

One little rabbit
Said he was tired
Walkin' down the road
Walkin' down the road
One little rabbit
Said he was tired
Walkin' down the road
To call on old friend toad.

So
Seven little rabbits
Turned around
Until they found

Down in the ground
A hole
Built by a mole.

Seven little rabbits
Went down the hole
Built by the mole
Down in the ground
Until they found
A den.

Then
The seventh little rabbit
Went to sleep—
Now don't say "Peep"—
He's tucked in bed
And now instead

Six little rabbits
Walkin' down the road
Walkin' down the road
Six little rabbits
Walkin' down the road
To call on old friend toad.

14

One little rabbit
Said he was tired
Walkin' down the road
Walkin' down the road
One little rabbit
Said he was tired
Walkin' down the road
To call on old friend toad.

So
Six little rabbits
Turned around
Until they found
Down in the ground
A hole
Built by a mole.

Six little rabbits
Went down the hole
Built by the mole
Down in the ground
Until they found
A den.

Then
The sixth little rabbit
Went to sleep—
Now don't say "Peep"—
He's tucked in bed
And now instead

Five little rabbits
Walkin' down the road
Walkin' down the road
Five little rabbits
Walkin' down the road
To call on old friend toad.

One little rabbit
Said he was tired
Walkin' down the road
Walkin' down the road
One little rabbit
Said he was tired
Walkin' down the road
To call on old friend toad.

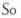

So
Five little rabbits
Turned around
Until they found
Down in the ground
A hole
Built by a mole.

Five little rabbits
Went down the hole
Built by the mole
Down in the ground
Until they found
A den.

Then
The fifth little rabbit
Went to sleep—
Now don't say "Peep"—
He's tucked in bed
And now instead

Four little rabbits
Walkin' down the road
Walkin' down the road
Four little rabbits
Walkin' down the road
To call on old friend toad.

One little rabbit
Said he was tired
Walkin' down the road
Walkin' down the road
One little rabbit
Said he was tired
Walkin' down the road
To call on old friend toad.

So
Four little rabbits
Turned around
Until they found
Down in the ground
A hole
Built by a mole.

Four little rabbits
Went down the hole
Built by the mole
Down in the ground
Until they found
A den.

Then
The fourth little rabbit
Went to sleep—
Now don't say "Peep"—
He's tucked in bed
And now instead

Three little rabbits
Walkin' down the road
Walkin' down the road
Three little rabbits
Walkin' down the road
To call on old friend toad.

One little rabbit
Said he was tired
Walkin' down the road
Walkin' down the road
One little rabbit
Said he was tired
Walkin' down the road
To call on old friend toad.

So
Three little rabbits
Turned around
Until they found
Down in the ground
A hole
Built by a mole.

Three little rabbits
Went down the hole
Built by the mole
Down in the ground
Until they found
A den.

Then
The third little rabbit
Went to sleep—
Now don't say "Peep"—
He's tucked in bed
And now instead

Two little rabbits
Walkin' down the road
Walkin' down the road
Two little rabbits
Walkin' down the road
To call on old friend toad.

One little rabbit
Said he was tired
Walkin' down the road
Walkin' down the road
One little rabbit
Said he was tired
Walkin' down the road
To call on old friend toad.

So
Two little rabbits
Turned around
Until they found
Down in the ground
A hole
Built by a mole.

Two little rabbits
Went down the hole
Built by the mole
Down in the ground
Until they found
A den.

Then
The second little rabbit
Went to sleep—
Now don't say "Peep"—
He's tucked in bed
And now instead

One little rabbit
Walkin' down the road
Walkin' down the road
One little rabbit
Walkin' down the road
To call on old friend toad.

One little rabbit
Said he was tired
Walkin' down the road
Walkin' down the road
One little rabbit
Said he was tired
Walkin' down the road
To call on old friend toad.

So
One little rabbit
Turned around
Until he found
Down in the ground
A hole
Built by a mole

One little rabbit
Went down the hole
Built by the mole
Down in the ground
Until he found
A den.

Then
The first little rabbit
Who was also the last
Went to sleep—
Now don't say "Peep"—
He's tucked in bed
And now instead
Of walkin' down the road
Of walkin' down the road

The first little rabbit
Dreamed a dream
And to him it seemed
All in a blur
As if there were

21

Seven little rabbits
Walkin' down the road
Walkin' down the road
Seven little rabbits
Walkin' down the road
To call on old friend toad.

—*John Becker*

If You Ever

The leader should recite this alone once. When the children recognize the rhythm, they will chime in.

If you ever ever ever ever ever
    If you ever ever ever meet a whale
You must never never never never never
    You must never never never touch its tail:
For if you ever ever ever ever ever
    If you ever ever ever touch its tail,
You will never never never never never
    You will never never meet another whale.

What Did You Put in Your Pocket?

The audience joins in each refrain.

What did you put in your pocket
What did you put in your pocket
  in your pockety pockety pocket
Early Monday morning?

I put in some chocolate pudding
I put in some chocolate pudding
    slushy glushy pudding
Early Monday morning.

    Refrain: SLUSHY GLUSHY PUDDING!

What did you put in your pocket
What did you put in your pocket
    in your pockety pockety pocket
Early Tuesday morning?

I put in some ice-cold water
I put in some ice-cold water
    nicy icy water
Early Tuesday morning.

    Refrain: SLUSHY GLUSHY PUDDING!
             NICY ICY WATER!

What did you put in your pocket
What did you put in your pocket
    in your pockety pockety pocket
Early Wednesday morning?

I put in a scoop of ice cream
I put in a scoop of ice cream
    slurpy glurpy ice cream
Early Wednesday morning.

    Refrain: SLUSHY GLUSHY PUDDING!

          NICY ICY WATER!

          SLURPY GLURPY ICE CREAM!

What did you put in your pocket
What did you put in your pocket
    in your pockety pockety pocket
Early Thursday morning?

I put in some mashed potatoes
I put in some mashed potatoes
    fluppy gluppy potatoes
Early Thursday morning.

Refrain: SLUSHY GLUSHY PUDDING!
NICY ICY WATER!
SLURPY GLURPY ICE CREAM!
FLUPPY GLUPPY POTATOES!

What did you put in your pocket
What did you put in your pocket
    in your pockety pockety pocket
Early Friday morning?

I put in some sticky molasses
I put in some sticky molasses
    sticky icky molasses
Early Friday morning.

Refrain: SLUSHY GLUSHY PUDDING!
NICY ICY WATER!
SLURPY GLURPY ICE CREAM!
FLUPPY GLUPPY POTATOES!
STICKY ICKY MOLASSES!

What did you put in your pocket
What did you put in your pocket
    in your pockety pockety pocket
Early Saturday morning?

I put in my five fingers
I put in my five fingers
   funny finny fingers
Early Saturday morning.

> *Refrain:* SLUSHY GLUSHY PUDDING!
>   NICY ICY WATER!
>   SLURPY GLURPY ICE CREAM!
>   FLUPPY GLUPPY POTATOES!
>   STICKY ICKY MOLASSES!
>   FUNNY FINNY FINGERS!

What did you put in your pocket
What did you put in your pocket
   in your pockety pockety pocket
Early Sunday morning?

I put in a clean white handkerchief
I put in a clean white handkerchief
   a spinky spanky handkerchief
Early Sunday morning.

Refrain: SLUSHY GLUSHY PUDDING!

NICY ICY WATER!

SLURPY GLURPY ICE CREAM!

FLUPPY GLUPPY POTATOES!

STICKY ICKY MOLASSES!

FUNNY FINNY FINGERS!

SPINKY SPANKY HANDKERCHIEF!

—*Beatrice Schenk de Regniers*

Fire! Fire!

It's fun to make up different rhyming endings for this familiar verse. The leader may omit the last word of each line and let the listeners supply the rhyme.

"Fire! Fire!"
Cried Mrs. _____ (McGuire)

"Where? Where?"
Cried Mrs. _____ (Blair)

"All over town!"
Cried Mrs. _____ (Brown)

"Get some water!"
Cried Mrs. _____ (Potter)

"We'd better jump!"
Cried Mrs. _____ (Gump)

"That would be silly!"
Cried Mrs. _____ (Brunilly)

"It looks too risky!"
Cried Mrs. _____ (Matriski)

"What'll we do?"
Cried Mrs. _____ (La Rue)

"Turn in an alarm!"
Cried Mrs. _____ (La Farme)

"Save us! Save us!"
Cried Mrs. _____ (Potayvus)

31

Adventures of Isabel

As the leader recites this, the listeners should repeat the refrain.

Isabel met an enormous bear,
Isabel, Isabel didn't care;
The bear was hungry, the bear was ravenous,
The bear's mouth was cruel and cavernous.
The bear said, Isabel, glad to meet you,
How do, Isabel, now I'll eat you!
Isabel, Isabel, didn't worry,
Isabel didn't scream or scurry.
She washed her hands and she straightened her hair up,
Then Isabel quietly ate the bear up.

Once in a night as black as pitch
Isabel met a wicked witch.
The witch's face was cross and wrinkled,
The witch's gums with teeth were sprinkled.
Ho ho, Isabel! the old witch crowed,
I'll turn you into an ugly toad!
Isabel, Isabel, didn't worry,
Isabel didn't scream or scurry,
She showed no rage and she showed no rancor,
But she turned the witch into milk and drank her.

—*Ogden Nash*

The Toaster

*For full enjoyment of this poem, do not reveal the title; read the
poem and ask for guesses as to what it's about.*

A silver-scaled Dragon with jaws flaming red
Sits at my elbow and toasts my bread.
I hand him fat slices, and then, one by one,
He hands them back when he sees they are done.

—*William Jay Smith*

This Man Had Six Eyes

*To make this doubly enjoyable, do not read all of the last line;
give the children time to guess the identity of the "man."*

I met a man that had six eyes
And still he could not see.
He lay in bed and hid his head
And would not look at me.

I pulled him up and took him home
(I don't think I did wrong.)
And I let him stay, and day by day
I saw his eyes grow long.

I saw them grow out of his head.
I saw them turn to me.
I saw them grow a foot or so.
And *still* he could not see.

"I think he could see the sun," I said,
So I put him on the sill,
And gave him a drink. But what do you think?
His eyes kept growing still.

They grew as long as I was tall.
They grew like a sleepy tree.
They grew to the floor and out the door.
And still they could not see.

Now what do you think has eyes that long?
You may tell me now if you know.
Or look in the pot: there, like as not,
You will find . . . MR. POT 8 OH!

—*John Ciardi*

Poor Old Lady Swallowed a Fly

Although this may also be sung, it is equally effective for a group to recite together. Leader starts; children follow.

Poor old lady, she swallowed a fly.
I don't know why she swallowed a fly.
Poor old lady, I think she'll die.

Poor old lady, she swallowed a spider.
It squirmed and wriggled and turned inside her.
She swallowed the spider to catch the fly.
I don't know why she swallowed a fly.
Poor old lady, I think she'll die.

Poor old lady, she swallowed a bird.
How absurd! She swallowed a bird.
She swallowed the bird to catch the spider,
She swallowed the spider to catch the fly.
I don't know why she swallowed a fly.
Poor old lady, I think she'll die.

Poor old lady, she swallowed a cat.
Think of that! She swallowed a cat.
She swallowed the cat to catch the bird.
She swallowed the bird to catch the spider.
She swallowed the spider to catch the fly.
I don't know why she swallowed a fly.
Poor old lady, I think she'll die.

Poor old lady, she swallowed a dog.
She went the whole hog when she swallowed the dog.
She swallowed the dog to catch the cat,
She swallowed the cat to catch the bird,
She swallowed the bird to catch the spider.
She swallowed the spider to catch the fly,
I don't know why she swallowed a fly.
I think she'll die.

Poor old lady, she swallowed a cow.
I don't know how she swallowed the cow.
She swallowed the cow to catch the dog,
She swallowed the dog to catch the cat,
She swallowed the cat to catch the bird,
She swallowed the bird to catch the spider,
She swallowed the spider to catch the fly,
I don't know why she swallowed a fly.
Poor old lady, I think she'll die.

Poor old lady, she swallowed a horse.
She died, of course.

—*Rose Bonne*

Limericks

There once was a boy of Bagdad,
An inquisitive sort of a lad.
    He said, "I will see
    If a sting has a bee."
And he very soon found that it had!

A flea and a fly in a flue
Were caught, so what could they do:
    Said the fly, "Let us flee."
    "Let us fly," said the flea.
So they flew through a flaw in the flue.

There once was a plesiosaurus
Which lived when the earth was all porous.
But it fainted with shame
When it first heard its name,
And departed long ages before us.

An oyster from Kalamazoo
Confessed he was feeling quite blue,
"For," says he, "as a rule,
When the weather turns cool,
I invariably get in a stew!"

A sleeper from the Amazon
Put nighties of his gra'mazon—
The reason, that
He was too fat
To get his own pajamazon.

Antonio

Read this once slowly and with exaggerated concern; on second reading, invite the audience to join in, if they do not do so spontaneously.

Antonio, Antonio,
Was tired of living alonio.
    He thought he would woo
    Miss Lissamy Loo
Miss Lissamy Lucy Molonio.

Antonio, Antonio,
Rode off on his polo-polonio.
    He found the fair maid
    In a bowery shade,
A-sitting and knitting alonio.

Antonio, Antonio,
Said, "If you will be my ownio,
    I'll love you true,
    And I'll buy for you,
An icery creamery conio!"

"Oh, Nonio, Antonio! . .
You're far too bleak and bonio!
    And all that I wish,
    You singular fish,
Is that you will quickly begonio."

Antonio, Antonio,
He uttered a dismal moanio;
    Then ran off and hid
    (Or I'm told that he did)
In the Anticatarctical Zonio.

—*Laura E. Richards*

STORIES

These are all audience-participation and action stories of one kind or another. Some might even be called action games. In order to enjoy them fully, sing out the refrains and repetitions along with the leader. If you read them by yourself, shout them out anyway.

Where the story calls for repeated actions, follow the leader carefully. You will discover how much more fun it is when anyone makes a mistake.

The Yellow Ribbon

A catch tale. It may be expanded or shortened to fit the mood and available time; it's shrinkable or stretchable!

ONCE there was a boy named John and a girl named Jane. John loved Jane very much. They lived next door to each other, and they went to first grade together, and John did love Jane very much. Every day John would carry Jane's books to school and every day Jane wore a yellow ribbon around her neck.

One day John said, "Jane, why do you wear that yellow ribbon around your neck?"

"I can't tell," said Jane, "and anyway I don't feel like telling you." But John kept asking, and finally Jane said maybe she'd tell him later sometime.

The next year John and Jane were in the second grade. One day John asked again, "Janey, why do you wear that yellow ribbon around your neck?"

"It's not really your affair, John; maybe I'll tell you sometime . . . but not now," said Jane.

Time went by; John still loved Jane and Jane loved John. And John carried Jane's books to school and Jane wore the yellow ribbon around her neck. They were in the fourth grade . . . then came the sixth grade . . . then junior high school. And every once in a while John asked Jane why she wore the yellow ribbon, but Jane never told. "We've been friends a long time, John, what difference does it make?" she said. And so time went by.

John and Jane went through high school together. John still loved Jane and Jane loved John. John carried Jane's books to school and Jane still wore the yellow ribbon around her neck. On graduation day John said, "Jane, we're being graduated now. Won't you *please* tell me why you wear that yellow ribbon around your neck?"

"Oh John," said Jane, "there's no point in telling you on graduation day . . . but someday I will." And that day passed.

Time went by, and John still loved Jane and Jane loved John and Jane still wore that yellow ribbon around her neck.

One day, John and Jane became engaged. John loved Jane and Jane loved John. "Why do you wear that yellow ribbon around your neck, Jane honey?" said John, and finally Jane said maybe she would tell him why on their wedding day.

But the wedding day came and what with all the preparations

for the wedding and the honeymoon and all, John just forgot to ask. But several days later, John asked Jane why she wore that yellow ribbon around her neck.

"Well, we are happily married and we love each other, so what difference does it make, John?" said Jane. So John let that pass, but he still *did* want to know.

Time went by. John loved Jane and Jane loved John. Lovely children were born to them, and they were so busy bringing them up that before they knew it, it was their golden wedding anniversary.

"Jane, why do you wear that yellow ribbon around your neck?" asked John once more. And Jane said, "Since you have waited this long, you can wait a little longer. I'll tell you someday, John."

Time went by. John loved Jane and Jane loved John. Finally Jane was taken very ill and was dying. John bent on his knees by her bedside, and with sobs in his voice, asked, "Janey, *please* tell me: Why do you wear that yellow ribbon around your neck?"

"All right, John. You may untie it now," said Jane.

So John did . . . AND JANE'S HEAD FELL OFF!

—*Maria Leach*

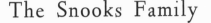

The Snooks Family

An audience-participation story. Follow the leader!

ONE NIGHT Mr. and Mrs. Snooks were going to bed as usual. It so happened that Mrs. Snooks got into bed first, and she said to her husband, "Please, Mr. Snooks, would you blow the candle out?"

And Mr. Snooks replied, "Certainly, Mrs. Snooks." Whereupon he picked up the candlestick and began to blow, but unfortunately he could only blow by putting his under lip over his upper lip, which meant that his breath went up to the ceiling instead of blowing out the candle flame.

And he puffed and he puffed and he puffed, but he could not blow it out.

So Mrs. Snooks said, "I will do it, my dear," and she got out of bed and took the candlestick from her husband and began to blow. But unfortunately she could only blow by putting her upper lip over her under lip, so that all her breath went down onto the floor. And she puffed and she puffed, but she could not blow the candle out.

So Mrs. Snooks called their son John. John put on his sky-blue dressing gown and slipped his feet into his primrose-colored slippers and came down into his parents' bedroom.

"John, dear," said Mrs. Snooks, "will you please blow out the candle for us?"

And John said, "Certainly, Mummy."

But unfortunately John could only blow out of the right corner of his mouth, so that all his breath hit the wall of the room instead of the candle.

And he puffed and he puffed, but he could not blow out the candle.

So they all called for his sister, little Ann. And little Ann put on her scarlet dressing gown and slipped on her pink slippers and came down to her parents' bedroom.

"Ann, dear," said Mr. Snooks, "will you please blow the candle out for us?"

And Ann said, "Certainly, Daddy."

But unfortunately Ann could only blow out of the left side of her mouth, so that all her breath hit the wall instead of the candle.

And she puffed and she puffed and she puffed, but she could not blow out the candle.

It was just then that they heard in the street below a heavy, steady tread coming along the pavement. Mr. Snooks threw open

the window and they all craned their heads out. They saw a policeman coming slowly towards the house.

"Oh, Mr. Policeman," said Mrs. Snooks, "will you come up
and blow out our candle? We do so want to go to bed."

"Certainly, Madam," replied the policeman, and he entered
and climbed the stairs—blump, blump, blump. He came into the
bedroom where Mr. Snooks, Mrs. Snooks, John Snooks and little
Ann Snooks were standing around the candle which they could
NOT blow out.

The policeman then picked up the candlestick in a very dignified
manner and, putting his mouth into the usual shape for blowing,
puffed out the candle at the first puff. Just like this—PUFF!

Then the Snooks family all said, "Thank you, Mr. Policeman."

And the policeman said, "Don't mention it," and turned to go down the stairs again.

"Just a moment, Policeman," said Mr. Snooks. "You mustn't go down the stairs in the dark. You might fall." And taking a box of matches, he LIT THE CANDLE AGAIN!

Mr. Snooks went down the stairs with the policeman and saw him out of the door. His footsteps went blump, blump, blump along the quiet street.

John Snooks and little Ann Snooks went back to bed. Mr. and Mrs. Snooks got into bed again. There was silence for a moment.

"Mr. Snooks," said Mrs. Snooks, "would you blow out the candle?"

Mr. Snook got out of bed. "Certainly, Mrs. Snooks," he said . . .

And so on AD INFINITUM.

—*Harcourt Williams*

The Hobyahs

Start the first "Hobyah! Hobyah! Hobyah! Tear down the hempstalks. Eat up the old man. Eat up the old woman. Carry off the little girl!" in a soft voice. Then the audience should join in and each successive cry should become louder until the end is very loud and shrill.

ONCE there was an old man and an old woman and a little girl and they all lived in a house made of hempstalks. Now the old man had a little dog named Turpie; and one night the Hobyahs came and said, "Hobyah! Hobyah! Hobyah! Tear down the hempstalks. Eat up the old man. Eat up the old woman. Carry off the little girl!" But little dog Turpie barked so that the Hobyahs ran off. And the old man said, "Little dog Turpie barks so that I can neither slumber nor sleep, and if I live till morning I will cut off his tail."

So in the morning the old man cut off little dog Turpie's tail.

The next night the Hobyahs came again, and said, "Hobyah! Hobyah! Hobyah! Tear down the hempstalks. Eat up the old man. Eat up the old woman. Carry off the little girl!" But little dog Turpie barked so that the Hobyahs ran off; and the old man said, "Little dog Turpie barks so that I can neither slumber nor sleep, and if I live till morning I will cut off one of his legs."

So in the morning the old man cut off one of little dog Turpie's legs.

The next night the Hobyahs came again, and said, "Hobyah! Hobyah! Hobyah! Tear down the hempstalks. Eat up the old man. Eat up the old woman. Carry off the little girl!" But little dog Turpie barked so that the Hobyahs ran off; and the old man said, "Little dog Turpie barks so that I can neither slumber nor sleep, and if I live till morning I will cut off another of his legs."

So in the morning the old man cut off another of little dog Turpie's legs.

The next night the Hobyahs came again, and said, "Hobyah! Hobyah! Hobyah! Tear down the hempstalks. Eat up the old man. Eat up the old woman. Carry off the little girl!" But little dog Turpie barked so that the Hobyahs ran off; and the old man said, "Little dog Turpie barks so that I can neither slumber nor sleep, and if I live till morning I will cut off another of his legs."

So in the morning the old man cut off another of little dog Turpie's legs.

The next night the Hobyahs came again, and said, "Hobyah!

Hobyah! Hobyah! Tear down the hempstalks. Eat up the old man. Eat up the old woman. Carry off the little girl!'' But little dog Turpie barked so that the Hobyahs ran off; and the old man said, "Little dog Turpie barks so that I can neither slumber nor sleep, and if I live till morning I will cut off another of his legs."

So in the morning the old man cut off another of little dog Turpie's legs.

The next night the Hobyahs came again, and said, "Hobyah! Hobyah! Hobyah! Tear down the hempstalks. Eat up the old man. Eat up the old woman. Carry off the little girl!" But little dog Turpie barked so that the Hobyahs ran off; and the old man said, "Little dog Turpie barks so that I can neither slumber nor sleep and if I live till morning, I will cut off little dog Turpie's HEAD!''

So in the morning the old man cut off little dog Turpie's head.

The next night the Hobyahs came again, and said, "Hobyah! Hobyah! Hobyah! Tear down the hempstalks. Eat up the old man. Eat up the old woman. Carry off the little girl!" But this time little dog Turpie did not bark, and when the Hobyahs found that little dog Turpie's head was off they tore down the hempstalks, ate up the old man, ate up the old woman, and carried off the little girl in a bag.

And when the Hobyahs came to their home they hung up the bag with the little girl in it, and every Hobyah knocked on the top of the bag and said, "Look me! Look me!" And they went to sleep until the next night because the Hobyahs sleep in the daytime.

The little girl cried a great deal and a man with a big dog came that way and heard her crying. When he asked her how she came there and she told him, he put the dog in the bag and took the little girl to his home.

The next night the Hobyahs took down the bag and knocked on the top of it, and said, "Look me! Look me!" and when they opened the bag——the big dog jumped out and ate them all up, every single one.

So-o-o-o—there are no Hobyahs left in the world now!

Sody Saleratus

Be sure to say the "I'll eat you up" lines in unison.

ONE TIME there was an old woman and an old man and a little boy and a little girl—and a frisky pet squirrel sittin' up on the fireboard. And one day the old woman wanted to bake some biscuits but she didn't have no sody, so she sent the little boy off to the store for sody sallyratus. The little boy he went trottin' on down the road singin', "Sody, sody, sody, sallyratus!" Trotted across the bridge and on to the store and got the sody sallyratus, and started trottin' on back.

Got to the bridge and started across and an old bear stuck his head out from under it, says:

"I'LL EAT YOU UP—YOU AND YOUR SODY SALLYRATUS!"

So he swallered the little boy—him and his sody sallyratus.

The old woman and the old man and the little girl and the frisky pet squirrel they waited and they waited for the little boy, but he didn't come and didn't come, so finally the old woman sent the little girl after the little boy. She skipped down the road and skipped across the bridge and on to the store, and the storekeeper told her the little boy had already been there and gone. So she started skippin' back, and when she got to the bridge the old bear stuck his head out—

"I EAT A LITTLE BOY—HIM AND HIS SODY SALLYRATUS—AND
I'LL EAT YOU TOO!"

So he swallered her down.

The old woman and the old man and the frisky pet squirrel
they waited and they waited but the little girl didn't come and
didn't come, so the old woman sent the old man after the little boy
and the little girl. He walked on down the road, walked across
the bridge—KARUMP! KARUMP! KARUMP!—and walked on till
he came to the store, and the storekeeper told him the little boy
and the little girl had already been there and gone.

"They must'a stopped somewhere 'side the road to play."

So the old man he started walkin' on back. Got to the bridge—

"I EAT A LITTLE BOY, HIM AND HIS SODY SALLYRATUS, AND I EAT A LITTLE GIRL—AND I'LL EAT YOU, TOO!"

And the old bear reached and grabbed the old man and swallered him.

Well, the old woman and the frisky pet squirrel they waited and waited but the old man didn't come and didn't come. So the old woman SHE put out a-hunchety-hunchin' down the road, crossed the bridge, got to the store, and the storekeeper told her, says, "That boy's already done been here and gone—him and the little girl and the old man, too."

So the old woman she went hunchin' on back—a-hunchety-hunchety-hunch. Got to the bridge—

"I EAT A LITTLE BOY, HIM AND HIS SODY SALLYRATUS, AND I EAT A LITTLE GIRL, AND I EAT AN OLD MAN—AND I'LL EAT YOU, TOO!"

Reached out and grabbed her, and swallered HER up.

Well, the frisky pet squirrel he waited and he waited and he waited, and he went to runnin' back and forth up there on the fireboard, and he was gettin' hungrier and hungrier; so finally he jumped down on the table, jumped off on the bench and jumped to the floor. Shook his tail out behind him and out the door and down the road, just a-friskin'. Scuttered across the bridge and on in the store. R'ared up on his hindquarters and looked for the storekeeper, squarked a time or two, and when the storekeeper looked up and saw him, the pet squirrel raised up on his tiptoes and asked him had he seen anything of the little boy or the little girl or the old man or the old woman.

"Law, yes! They all done already been here and gone. Surely they ain't ALL done stopped 'side the road to play."

So the pet squirrel he stretched his tail out behind him and frisked out the door. Frisked on over the bridge—

"I EAT A LITTLE BOY, HIM AND HIS SODY SALLYRATUS, AND I EAT A LITTLE GIRL, AND I EAT AN OLD MAN, AND I EAT AN OLD WOMAN —AND I'LL EAT YOU, TOO!"

The little frisky pet squirrel he stuck his tail straight up in the air and just chittered, but time the old bear made for him he was already scratchin' halfway up a tree. The old bear he went clamberin' up to get him. The squirrel got 'way out on a limb, and the old bear started out the limb after him. The squirrel he jumped and caught in the next tree.

"HUMPF! IF YOU CAN MAKE IT WITH YOUR LITTLE LEGS, I *know* I CAN MAKE IT WITH MY BIG 'UNS!"

And the old bear tried to jump—didn't quite make it. Down he went and when he hit the ground he split wide open.

The old woman stepped out, and the old man he stepped out, and the little girl jumped, and the little boy he jumped out. And the old woman says, "Where's my sody sallyratus?"

"Here," says the little boy, and he handed it to her.

So they went on back to the house and the frisky pet squirrel he scooted on ahead of 'em, cloomb back up on the fireboard and curled his tail over his back, and watched the old woman till she took the biscuits out the oven. So then she broke him off a chunk and blew on it till it wasn't too hot, and handed it up to him. And he took it in his forepaws and turned it over and over and nibbled on it—and when he eat it up he leaned down and chittered for some more. And he was so hungry the old woman had to hand him chunks till he'd eat two whole biscuits.

—Richard Chase

The Busy Farmer's Wife

The leader tells the story and demonstrates the actions. Children imitate the actions. Each motion, once started, is continued after the next one begins so that, by the end of the story, all motions are going on at once.

The farmer's wife has many duties. She keeps busy all day long. The other day I visited a friend of mine and found her in the kitchen. She was standing at the stove stirring a big pot of apple butter.

(Make stirring motion with right hand.)

The churn was standing nearby and she was pumping the handle up and down as she stirred the apple butter.

(Make pumping motion up and down with left hand; continue stirring motion with the right hand.)

One of the girls came in with a piece of taffy she had made at a taffy party, and put a piece in her mother's mouth. So there my friend stood, stirring and pumping the churn and chewing.

> (*Make chewing motion with mouth*
> *while continuing other motions.*)

All of a sudden she noticed that the screen door had been left open and the chickens were coming in the kitchen. She couldn't leave her churning and the apple butter, so all she could do was stand there shaking her head at the chickens and yelling, "Shoo, shoo, shoo."

> (*Move head up and down as if gesturing*
> *toward the door while making shooing sounds.*
> *Continue all other motions.*)

61

The Lion Hunt

Lion hunting is dangerous; thus, it is necessary to stay together. Group must repeat everything exactly as the leader says it and does it.

LEADER: Do you WANT to go on a lion hunt?
> *(Children may answer in various ways. Leader reminds children they must repeat her words and actions exactly.)*

CHILDREN: Do you WANT to go on a lion hunt?

LEADER: Well, then, let's go.

CHILDREN: Well, then, let's go.

This pattern of repetition of EVERY line and action continues throughout the whole story.

Let's start walking.
   (*Make walking sounds with feet on floor.*)

We'll have to cross a bridge.
   (*Hit palms on thighs to simulate sound of feet on bridge.*)

Now we're across the bridge.

Horses are waiting for us here.

We'll ride part of the way.
   (*Hold reins in hands. Bounce up and down. Make clucking sounds with tongue to simulate sound of horses hooves on ground. Give occasional "giddap."*)

This is as far as we can go with the horses.

We'll have to walk from here.
   (*Make walking sounds with feet.*)

Oh! It's beginning to rain.
   (*Rub palms together in circular motion to make sounds of rain.*)

It's getting muddy.

We'll have to walk in the mud.

It's hard going.
   (*Make claws of hands, turn palms down and make motions in walking rhythm as if pulling feet in mud. Make juicy, slurpy sound with mouth.*)

In fact, we're walking through a bog.
> (*Continue slurping sound and same motions.*)

The mosquitoes are biting.
> (*Slap at face and neck; scratch here and there; continue slurping walk through bog.*)

We're finally on dry ground now.

We can walk a little faster.
> (*Make walking sounds with feet.*)

Oh, oh, wait a minute.

I think I see something.
> (*Hold hand to eye.*)

Yes, I see a stream.

Shall we take a run?

And jump over it?

Ready?

Let's go.
> (*Make running rhythm, slapping palms on thighs. Raise palms in midair, hold for a moment, hit thighs again, simulating sounds of a jump over the stream.*)

We made it!

We'll have to walk through the reeds.
  (*Put hands in front of face to separate reeds which block passage.*)

Now we're on clear ground again.
  (*Make walking sounds with hands slapping thighs.*)

Stop!

Wait a minute.

I see a big river.

Let's take a long run.

And a big jump.

If we don't make it, we'll have to swim.

Ready?

Run!
  (*Make running rhythm, slapping palms on thighs. Raise hands and hold in midair for a moment.*)

We'll never make it.

We'll have to swim.
  (*Hold nose with hands as if diving into water. Make spluttering noises. Begin swimming strokes.*)

We can walk the rest of the way.
  (*Make slurping sounds; pretend to walk in slow, painful crawl.*)

Well, we made it to shore.
> (*Wring out clothes and hair and shake self.*)

It ought to be easier from here on.

Let's go.
> (*Make walking rhythm with feet.*)

Hold it.
> (*Put hand to eyes.*)

I see a cave.

Shall we go in?

Careful now, here we go.
> (*Cup hands to mouth once inside cave.*)

It's dark in here.

I wonder if there's anyone here.

Yoo hoo.
> (*Louder.*)

I hear an echo.

Yooooooo. Hooooooo.

Hey.

I just happened to think of something.

There may be bears in here.

Let's get out of here.
  (*Make running sounds with feet.*)

Phew.

I'm glad we got out of there safely.

We'll have to climb this hill.
  (*Make slow walking rhythm.*)

It's getting steeper and steeper.

We'll have—to—go—slower—and slower.

Phew.

We're almost to the top.

Just a little farther.
  (*Make footsteps slower and slower.*)

Now we're at the top.

Let's rest a minute.

Take a deep breath.
  (*Take a loud sniff.*)

Isn't the air wonderful?
  (*Hit hands on chest.*)

Makes you feel so good.

Look at the beautiful view.

> (*Put hands to eyes, turning complete circle as though looking around.*)

Everybody rested?

Shall we run down the hill?

Ready?

Get set.

Go!

> (*Make running rhythm with feet on floor.*)

Shhhhhhhhhhhhhhh.

> (*Put finger to mouth.*)

We're near lion country.

We'll walk through this tall grass.

Grass makes a swishing sound.

> (*Slap palms together in swishing, not clapping sound. Make swishing sound with mouth.*)

Stop.

> (*In whisper.*)

This is where I last saw a lion.

Let's climb a tree.

> (*Curve arms as if climbing tree. Move hands higher and higher.*)

Careful, don't fall, now.

Hold on tight.

Let's look in this direction.

See anything?

I don't see anything.

Let's look in this direction.
  (Hold tree with one hand, put other hand to eye.)

See anything?

I don't see anything.

Look over here.

Can you see anything?

I don't see anything.

Now look this way.

Shuuuuuuuuuush!

I think I see something.

It has two big eyes.

And a long tail.

It's waving back and for

Back and forth.

It looks like a lion.

It is a lion.

69

Hand me the gun.

I don't have the gun.

Do you have the gun?

YOU don't have the gun?

Let's get out of here.
   (*Make motion of sliding down the tree. Whole party retraces steps in a dash, running up the hill, down the hill, and into the cave.*)

Let's wait here.

The lion may not find us.

SHHHHHHHSH.

Now, carefully, let's tiptoe out.
   (*Make motion of tiptoe walking.*)

Now hurry!

   (*Retrace route in double-quick time, swimming the river, walking over hard ground, walking through the reeds, running and jumping the stream, walking over the dry ground, walking through the bog, walking in the mud, walking through the rain sounds, riding horses, walking over the bridge, and so on.*)

We made it.

But if I ever go lion hunting with you again, I'll be sure to take the gun.

You can get killed going hunting without a gun!

The Shopping Trip

The leader tells the story and accompanies it with motions. The audience mimics the motions. Each motion, once started, is continued after the next one begins so that before the end of the story, hands, feet, head and jaws are all in motion.

We're all going on a shopping trip in the big department store.
(*Name a local one.*)

We're going to buy a pair of scissors first.
(*Cutting motion with forefinger and middle finger of right hand.*)

We need a new set of steps for the back porch.

(Walking-up-steps motion with feet.)

There was a sale of rocking chairs so we bought one.

(Rocking motion back and forth in chair while walking with feet and cutting with fingers.)

We got thirsty walking around and put a big piece of bubble gum in our mouths.

(Make lump in cheek with tongue and begin chewing.)

At this moment our heads began to itch.

(Scratch heads and remember to continue all motions.)

The salesman came up to us and asked if we wanted to buy anything else and we all said, "No."

(Shake head from side to side and continue all motions.)

I Went to the Library

Storytellers often make up their own special games for the stretch period. In this one, each player in turn has his chance to name a book title, but he must repeat all the previously named titles to stay in the game. Those who cannot remember all previous titles are out; the last player wins the game. If the group is too large, a few at a time may be chosen to play.

LEADER: I went to the library and I read *Tom Sawyer*. (*Any title may be chosen.*)

FIRST PLAYER: I went to the library and I read *Tom Sawyer* and *Curious George*. (*Another title is added.*)

SECOND PLAYER: I went to the library and I read *Tom Sawyer* and *Curious George* and *Homer Price*. (*A third title is added.*)

THIRD PLAYER: I went to the library and I read *Tom Sawyer* and *Curious George* and *Homer Price* and *Treasure Island*. (*Four titles.*)

Game continues until each child has had a turn and goes on until only one child is left as winner.

FINGER PLAYS

Some of these finger plays are very well known. You may know others also, or you may want to make up your own.

Clap Your Hands

Carry out actions indicated by the rhyme. Other actions may be added at the suggestion of the children, such as "wiggle your ears," "touch your nose," or "make a fist."

Clap your hands, clap your hands,
Clap them just like me.

Touch your shoulders, touch your shoulders,
Touch them just like me.

Tap your knees, tap your knees,
Tap them just like me.

Shake your head, shake your head,
Shake them just like me.

Clap your hands, clap your hands,
Now let them quiet be.

74

My Hands

Two little hands so soft and white.
    (*Show hands.*)

This is the left; this is the right.
    (*Indicate each one.*)

Five little fingers standing on each,
    (*Show fingers.*)

So I can hold a plum or a peach.
    (*Curve fingers as if holding a plum.*)

But when I get as big as you,
    (*Point to a child in the group.*)

I'll show you what these hands can do.
    (*Show hands.*)

Hands on Shoulders

Carry out actions indicated by the rhyme.

Hands on shoulders, hands on knees,
Hands behind you, if you please;
Touch your shoulders, now your nose,
Now your hair and now your toes;
Hands up high in the air,
Down at your sides and touch your hair;
Hands up high as before,
Now clap your hands, one, two, three, four.

Who Feels Happy?

Who feels happy? Who feels gay?
All who do, clap their hands this way.
    (*Clap hands.*)

Who feels happy? Who feels gay?
All who do, nod their heads this way.
    (*Nod head.*)

Who feels happy? Who feels gay?
All who do, tap their shoulders this way.
    (*Tap shoulder with hand.*)

Further actions may be suggested by the children. "Tap your feet," "swing your arms," and other motions can be added.

Hands Up

Carry out actions indicated by the rhyme.

Reach for the ceiling
Touch the floor,
Stand up again,
Let's do more.
Touch your head,
Then your knee;
Up to your shoulder,
Like this, see.
Reach for the ceiling
Touch the floor.
That's all now—
There isn't anymore.

My Eyes Can See

My eyes can see.
>   (*Make "eyeglasses" with hands.*)

My mouth can talk.
>   (*Move thumb and index finger as if talking.*)

My ears can hear.
>   (*Cup hand and place it behind ear.*)

My feet can walk.
>   (*Make second and third fingers of right hand "walk."*)

My nose can smell.
>   (*Touch nose.*)

My teeth can bite.
>   (*Move fingers together and apart as if chewing.*)

My lids can flutter.
>   (*Hold hands up to eyes and flutter fingers.*)

My hands can write.
>   (*Pretend to hold pen and write.*)

But when the clock
Its time doth show,
I'll take some books
>   (*Pick up some books.*)

And away I'll go.
>   (*Wave good-bye.*)

The Teapot

I'm a little teapot, short and stout.
This is my handle,
    (Put one hand on hip.)
This is my spout.
    (Extend opposite hand outward and slant it down for spout.)
When I get all steamed up and shout,
Just tip me over and pour me out.
    (Bend body toward arm extended as spout.)

The Turtle

There was a little turtle.
He lived in a box.
> *(Put index finger of right hand in upward palm of left hand.)*

He swam in a puddle.
> *(Make circular motion as if in a puddle.)*

He climbed on the rocks.
> *(Climb over the fingertips for "rocks.")*

He snapped at a mosquito;
> *(Make snapping motion by raising and lowering fingers and
> thumb of right hand.)*

He snapped at a flea;
He snapped at a minnow;
He snapped at me.

He caught the mosquito.
> *(Clasp and unclasp as if catching something.)*

He caught the flea;
He caught the minnow;
But he didn't catch me.
> *(Point to self.)*

Eensy Weensy Spider

The eensy, weensy spider
   (Extend and curve right-hand fingers.)
Climbed up the waterspout.
    (Fingers climb, spider-fashion up the left arm.)
Down came the rain
    (Sweep hands down and open wide.)
And washed the spider out.
Out came the sun
    (Make big circle with arms over head.)
And dried up all the rain.
So eensy, weensy spider
    (Make spider with curved fingers.)
Climbed up the spout again.
    (Fingers of right hand climb up the left arm again.)

RIDDLES

Some of the riddles here are like puzzles; you must guess the answers. Other riddles have trick endings. You may have your own favorites which you will want to share with the rest of your group.

Transportation Problem

Once there was a man who was set the task of taking a wolf, a goat, and a cabbage across the river. When he came to the river, he found that the boat was so small it would hold one man and only ONE OTHER thing.

What was he to do? How could he take the wolf, the goat, and the cabbage over, one at a time, so that the wolf wouldn't eat the goat and the goat wouldn't eat the cabbage?

ANSWERS:

4. Go back and get the goat.
3. Take the wolf over (leaving the goat behind).
2. Take the cabbage over and take the goat back.
1. Take the goat over.

OR

4. Go back and get the goat.
3. Take the cabbage over (leaving the goat behind).
2. Take the wolf over and take the goat back.
1. Take the goat over.

Endless Riddles

LEADER: Pete and Repeat were walking down the
street. Suddenly Pete went away.
Who was left?

GROUP: Repeat.

LEADER: Pete and Repeat were walking down the
street. Suddenly Pete went away.
Who was left? (*in louder voice*)

GROUP: Repeat.

LEADER: PETE AND REPEAT WERE WALKING, etc.
(*very loud*)

Continue to repeat the riddle louder and louder and more impatiently until the group dissolves in laughter.

LEADER: 'E was the greatest man on earth.

GROUP: Who was?

LEADER: 'E was.

GROUP: Who was 'e?

LEADER: 'Arry 'Arrington.

GROUP: Who was 'Arry 'Arrington?

LEADER: 'E was the greatest man on earth.

GROUP: Who was?

Leader continues to repeat the riddle until group stops repeating the response of its own accord.

American Riddles

1. Fiery little captain
     Of early Pilgrim fame;
   Close friend of John Alden—
     Can you tell his name?

2. Two cousins who had the same last name
   Were very unlike, yet both won fame.
   Rough Rider was one, then President.
   The other, twelve years in the White House spent.

3. She who came to us from France
     Holds a torch high in her hand;
   Welcomes travelers from afar,
     Coming to our friendly land.

4. Known by a nickname, this scout of the West
   Chased hostile Indians, rode by Pony Express.

5. Like a famous President
       Was this great man's name;
   And the lowly peanut
       Helped to bring him fame.

6. What bus crossed the ocean?

7. What has 18 legs and catches flies?

8. Why does the Statue of Liberty stand in New York Harbor?

ANSWERS:

8. Because it cannot sit down.
7. A baseball team.
6. Columbus.
5. George Washington Carver.
4. Buffalo Bill.
3. Statue of Liberty.
2. Theodore Roosevelt; Franklin Roosevelt.
1. Captain Miles Standish.

More Riddles

Once there was a donkey in a field and on one side of the field stood a ten-foot wall. On the other side a wide deep river flowed, and along the third side ran a thick prickly hedge. On the fourth side a steep high cliff rose. In a field close by there was a heap of carrots. How did the donkey get to the carrots?

Most groups supply the following answers:

GROUP: Jump over the wall?

LEADER: No, it was too high.

GROUP: Swim the river?

LEADER: No, he couldn't swim.

GROUP: Push through the hedge?

LEADER: No, it was too thick and prickly.

GROUP: Climb the cliff?

LEADER: No, it was too steep.

GROUP (*correct answer*): Well, we don't know.

LEADER: Neither did the donkey.

1. What would happen very soon
   If you swallowed your cereal spoon?

2. Riddle me, riddle me, riddle me reet,
   When do elephants have eight feet?

3. What can you see
      Down in the lake?
   That's always free
      But that no one can take?

4. What do the children
      In China call
   Young yellow cats
      When they are small?

ANSWERS:

4. Kittens.
3. The moon.
2. When there are two elephants.
1. You couldn't stir your cereal.

SONGS

Here are some songs which you will enjoy singing and acting out. For more fun, you can make up your own words and actions for many of them.

Smoke Goes up the Chimney

This song may be sung on one note or made-up tune.

Oh, you push the damper in (*push right arm forward*)
And you pull the damper out (*pull arm back*)
And the smoke goes up the chimney (*make spiral motion*)
Just the same. Just the same (*wave right arm to side; wave left arm
    to side*)
And the smoke goes up the chimney just the same.

Sing song with all the motions.
*Repeat and be quiet on "push damper in" but make motion in
    rhythm.*
*Repeat and be quiet on "push damper in" and "pull the damper
    out" but make motions in rhythm.*
*Repeat and be quiet on "push damper in" and "pull the damper
    out" and the first "smoke goes up the chimney" but make
    motions in rhythm.*
Repeat and be quiet on all lines. Make motions.
The last time you sing, the only words will be:

    Oh, you (*motion*)
    And you (*motion*)
    And the (*motion*) (*motion*) (*motion*)
    And the (*motion*)

If You're Happy and You Know It

If you're happy and you know it, clap your hands,
  (*Clap clap*)
If you're happy and you know it, clap your hands,
  (*Clap clap*)
If you're happy and you know it, then the whole wide world will
  know it,
If you're happy and you know it, clap your hands.
  (*Clap, clap*)

Other verses may include all kinds of actions, such as:

| stamp your feet | wiggle your ears |
| touch your toes | cross your legs |

Today Is Monday

Today is Monday, today is Monday
Monday, string beans
All you hungry children
Come and eat it up.

Today is Tuesday, today is Tuesday
Tuesday, spaghetti
Monday, string beans
All you hungry children
Come and eat it up.

Today is Wednesday, today is Wednesday
Wednesday, zoooop
Tuesday, spaghetti
Monday, string beans
All you hungry children
Come and eat it up.

Today is Thursday, today is Thursday
Thursday, roast beef . . .
(*continue as in third verse*)

Today is Friday, today is Friday
Friday, fresh fish . . .
(*continue as in fourth verse*)

Today is Saturday, today is Saturday
Saturday, chicken . . .
(*continue as in fifth verse*)

Today is Sunday . . .
Sunday, ice cream . . .
(*continue as in sixth verse*)

You may wish to make up your own menu after the first time.

Bingo

FIRST TIME: *The leader sings song straight through.*

SECOND TIME: *The whole group repeats song but keeps silent on letter* B; *clap hands in rhythm instead of singing* B.

THIRD TIME: *Repeat song but keep silent on letters* B *and* I; *clap hands in rhythm instead of singing* B *and* I.

FOURTH TIME: *Repeat song but keep silent on letters* B *and* I *and* N; *clap hands in rhythm instead of singing* B, I, N.

Continue to repeat song, keeping silent on each successive letter. Final and sixth time will have five claps instead of singing BINGO.

There was a farmer had a dog;
And Bingo was his name, sir.
B I N G O, B I N G O
B I N G O
Bingo was his name, sir.

That farmer's dog at our back door;
Begging for a bone, sir.
B I N G O, B I N G O
B I N G O
Bingo was his name, sir.

I Wish I Was a Mole in the Ground

I wish I was a mole in the ground,
I wish I was a mole in the ground,
If I was a mole in the ground,
I'd root that mountain down,
And I wish I was a mole in the ground.

I wish I was a lizard in the spring,
I wish I was a lizard in the spring,
If I was a lizard in the spring,
I'd hear my sweetheart sing,
And I wish I was a lizard in the spring.

Sing the song through once or twice. Then ask individual children to make wishes. Make up a rhyme on the spur of the moment and continue the song. The following are some examples made up by children in a library story hour.

I wish I was a horse in the stable,
I wish I was a horse in the stable,
If I was a horse in the stable,
I'd canter when I was able,
I wish I was a horse in the stable.

I wish I was an ant in the grass,
I wish I was an ant in the grass,
If I was an ant in the grass,
I'd tickle a little lass,
I wish I was an ant in the grass.

I wish I was a bird in a tree,
I wish I was a bird in a tree,
If I was a bird in a tree,
I'd see what I could see,
I wish I was a bird in a tree.

My Bonnie Lies over the Ocean

My bonnie lies over the ocean,
My bonnie lies over the sea,
My bonnie lies over the ocean,
Oh, bring back my bonnie to me.

Bring back, bring back,
Oh, bring back my bonnie to me . . . to me.
Bring back, bring back,
Oh, bring back my bonnie to me.

1. *Sing the whole song through the first time with no motions.*
2. *Repeat the whole song a second time with the following motions for each word:*

> *"my"—point to self*
> *"bonnie"—make figure of a girl in the air with*
> *both hands*

"lies"—put hands together and make a circle with
   the arms to indicate a cradle or bed
"over"—point to faraway with hand motion
"ocean"—make ocean waves in wavy motion of the
   right hand
"sea"—make wavy motion with right hand, but
   with a choppy, sharper stroke to differenti-
   ate from "ocean."
"oh"—join thumbs and index fingers in round O
"bring"—make beckoning motion with right hand
"back"—touch back of left shoulder with right
   hand
"to"—hold up two fingers
"me"—point again to self

3. Go through the motions slowly with the group once or twice;
   then try whole song.

John Brown's Baby

John Brown's baby had a cold upon his chest,
John Brown's baby had a cold upon his chest,
John Brown's baby had a cold upon his chest,
And they rubbed him down with camphorated oil.

1. *Sing the whole song through the first time with no motions.*
2. *Repeat whole song a second time, but remain silent on the word "baby." Instead, join arms together to make a circle in the shape of a cradle with a baby in it. Rock cradle each time word "baby" occurs.*
3. *Repeat song a third time; remain silent on words "baby" and "cold." Make cradling motion on word "baby" and make a loud coughing sound in place of the word "cold."*

4. Repeat song a fourth time; remain silent on words "baby," "cold," and "chest." Substitute cradling motion for "baby"; substitute a loud cough for "cold"; substitute a tap on the chest with the right hand for the word "chest."

5. Repeat the whole song a fifth time; remain silent on words "baby," "cold," "chest," "rubbed." Substitute cradling motion for "baby"; substitute a cough for "cold"; substitute a tap on the chest for "chest"; substitute a rubbing motion on the stomach for "rubbed."

Mister Rabbit

Mister Rabbit, Mister Rabbit, your ears mighty long,
  (*Hold hands on top of head to make ears*)
Yes, my Lawd, they're put on wrong.
  (*Nod head in agreement*)

REFRAIN
Every little soul must shine, shine, shine,
  (*Wind fists away from the body in slow circular motion*)
Every little soul must shine, shine, shine.
  (*Wind fists in* FAST *circular motion toward yourself*)

Mister Rabbit, Mister Rabbit, your coat mighty gray,
(Pat arm as though patting coat of animal)
Yes, my Lawd, 'twas made that way.
(Nod head in agreement)

REFRAIN
Every little soul must shine, shine, shine,
(Wind fists away from the body in low circular motion)
Every little soul must shine, shine, shine.
(Wind fists in FAST circular motion toward yourself)

Mister Rabbit, Mister Rabbit, your feet mighty red,
(Point to feet; wiggle feet)
Yes, my Lawd, I'm almost dead.
(Close eyes, let body go limp as if dead, fold hands in prayer position)

REFRAIN: *same as above*

Mister Rabbit, Mister Rabbit, your tail mighty white,
(Make hand motions to indicate long tail)
Yes, my Lawd, and I'm a-getting out of sight.
(Close eyes with both palms of hands)

REFRAIN: *same as above*

One Finger Keep Moving

1. One finger keep moving,
    (Hold up right index finger and begin wiggling it)
One finger keep moving,
    (Wiggle finger again and stop)
One finger keep moving,
    (Start finger wiggling)
And we'll all be happy and gay.
    (Continue wiggling finger)

2. One finger
    (Hold up right index finger)
Two fingers,
    (Hold up left index finger)
Keep moving.
    (Wiggle both index fingers)
One finger,
    (Stop wiggling fingers; hold up right index finger)
Two fingers,
    (Show left index finger)
Keep moving.
    (Wiggle both fingers while singing)
One finger, two fingers keep moving,
    (Show right, then left forefingers and keep both wiggling)
And we'll all be happy and gay.
    (Wiggle both fingers)

3. One finger, two fingers, one thumb, two thumbs keep moving, etc.

> *(Continue the song by showing each part of the body mentioned and adding one portion at a time as the words dictate; during the singing of "And we'll all be happy and gay," all the accumulated motions must be kept going.)*

4. One finger, two fingers, one thumb, two thumbs, one arm, two arms keep moving, etc.

5. One finger, two fingers, one thumb, two thumbs, one arm, two arms, one foot, two feet, etc.

6. One finger, two fingers, one thumb, two thumbs, one arm, two arms, one foot, two feet, one head (nod head up and down), keep moving, etc.

7. One finger, two fingers, one thumb, two thumbs, one arm, two arms, one foot, two feet, one head, stand up, sit down, keep moving, etc.

John Jacob Jingleheimer Schmidt

Repeat this song as many times as you wish, each time more and more softly. Finally, the words are repeated silently until the last line, which is shouted as loudly as possible.

John Jacob Jingleheimer Schmidt!
His name is my name too;
Whenever we go out,
Hear the happy people shout;
John Jacob Jingleheimer Schmidt!
Ta ra ra ra ra ra ra

John Jacob Jingleheimer Schmidt!
His name is my name too;
Whenever we go out,
Hear the happy people shout;
John Jacob Jingleheimer Schmidt!
Ta ra ra ra ra ra ra

John Jacob Jingleheimer Schmidt!
His name is my name too;
Whenever we go out,
Hear the happy people shout;
John Jacob Jingleheimer Schmidt!
Ta ra ra ra ra ra ra

Put Your Finger in the Air

Act out motions as verses suggest.

Put your finger in the air, in the air,
Put your finger in the air, in the air,
Put your finger in the air. Tell me, how's the air up there?
Put your finger in the air, in the air.

Put your finger on your head, on your head,
    (Repeat)
Put your finger on your head. Tell me, is it green or red?
    (Repeat first line)

Put your finger on your cheek, on your cheek,
    (Repeat)
Put your finger on your cheek. Leave it there a week.
    (Repeat first line)

Put your finger on your nose, on your nose,
    (*Repeat*)
Put your finger on your nose. Is that where the cold wind blows?
    (*Repeat first line*)

Put your finger on your chest, on your chest,
    (*Repeat*)
Put your finger on your chest. Give it just a little rest.
    (*Repeat first line*)

Put your finger on your belly, on your belly,
    (*Repeat*)
Put your finger on your belly. Make it shake like apply jelly.
    (*Repeat first line*)

—*Woody Guthrie*

TONGUE TWISTERS AND JOKES

Many children have enjoyed the tongue twisters and nonsense jokes included here. You will have other favorites to share with your group.

SAY QUICKLY:

A schmoo slyly slowly shuffled a snorkle full of slush.

Billy Botter baked biscuits with bitter butter in the batter.

The rat ran over the ridge of the roof with a raw lump of liver in his mouth.

A big black bug bit a big black bear,
And made the big black bear bleed blood.

Sally Simpson sold the seashells Sandy saw sitting on the seashore.

Six long slim slick sycamore saplings.

NICE OLD LADY: And what are *you* going to do, Billy, when you get as big as your father?

BILLY: Go on a diet.

BOASTFUL BOB: My father is an Elk, a Lion and a Moose.

PRACTICAL PETE: So how much does it cost to see him?

BOB: What a terrible bump on your head! What did that?

SAM: Tomatoes.

BOB: Heavens! How could tomatoes cause a huge bump like that?

SAM: They were in a can!

TEACHER: What is a cannibal?

BOB: I don't know.

TEACHER: Well, what would you be if you ate your mother and father?

BOB: An orphan.

TEACHER: Tommy, your hands are very dirty. What would you say if I came to school with dirty hands?

TOMMY: I'd be too polite to mention it.

BILL: What can a five-ton elephant do?

JOE: A-N-Y-T-H-I-N-G he wants!

COLLECTOR'S NOTE TO STORYTELLERS

As all storytellers know, there comes a time during the formal story hour conducted in a public or school library, playground or classroom, when a change of pace, of tone and of mood is desirable in order to relax both storyteller and story listener.

In order to prevent monotony in the story hour, many storytellers vary the types of stories in any one listening session by including myths, hero tales, or folk stories from various cultures. They may also mix stories with poetry or folk songs or finger plays.

On the other hand, some storytellers prefer to build their story hours around one theme or mood, and rely on the form rather than the content of their material to provide variety.

In either case, about halfway through the program, a "stretch" period or a "break" is welcome. During this short five- to ten-minute period, both teller and listener can move tense muscles and relax intensive listening and telling by joining in short verbal exchanges that are fun to do in a group.

The "stretch" does not imply that the children are permitted to leave their seats—for to seat them again into a receptive listening mood may be difficult. The "break" should consist of stretching vocal muscles or hand and foot movements calculated to provide a change of pace. Baseball's seventh-inning stretch is based on this same sound principle.

The short, simple stories, songs, chants, rhymes and activities in this book have been used in the "stretch" by this storyteller with maximum success.

Acknowledgments

Grateful acknowledgment is made to the following publishers and individuals, for permission to reprint copyrighted material in this book:

Abelard-Schuman Limited for five riddles from *Riddles, Riddles Everywhere* by Ennis Rees, Copyright 1964 by Ennis Rees; and for two tongue twisters from *Rainbow in the Morning* by Carl Withers and Alta Jablow, Copyright 1956 by Carl Withers and Alta Jablow. All rights reserved. Reprinted by permission.

Abingdon Press for "Smoke Goes up the Chimney" from *Act It Out* by Bernice Wells Carlson, Copyright 1956 by Pierce and Washabaugh; and for eight American History riddles from *American Riddles in Rhyme* by Ruby B. Murphy, Copyright 1955 by Pierce and Washabaugh. Reprinted by permission.

The Bodley Head Limited for "The Snooks Family" from *Tales from Ebony* by Harcourt Williams, published by Nattali & Maurice, Ltd.

Mrs. Margaret G. Burroughs for "Head and Shoulders, Baby" and "Who Did?" from *Did You Feed My Cow?*, published by Thomas Y. Crowell Company in 1956.

The Clarendon Press, Oxford, for the basic story of "The Dark House" and for the riddle of the donkey from *The Lore and Language of Schoolchildren* by Iona and Peter Opie, 1959. Reprinted by permission.

Thomas Y. Crowell Company, New York, for five limericks from *Laughable Limericks* by Sara and John E. Brewton, Text copyright © 1965 by Sara and John E. Brewton. Reprinted by permission.

Doubleday & Company, Inc. for five jokes from *The Real Book of Jokes* by Margaret Gossett, Copyright 1954 by Franklin Watts, Inc. Reprinted by permission.

Carl Fischer, Inc. for the words and music of "I Wish I Was a Mole in the Ground," Copyright 1929 by Carl Fischer, Inc., New York. Reprinted by permission.

Folkways Music Publishers, Inc. for the words and music of "Put Your Finger in the Air" by Woody Guthrie, © Copyright 1954 by Folkways Music Publishers, Inc., New York, N.Y. Reprinted by permission.

Harcourt, Brace & World, Inc. for "What Did You Put in Your Pocket" from *Something Special* by Beatrice Schenk de Regniers, Text © 1958 by Beatrice Schenk de Regniers. Reprinted by permission.

Harper & Row, Publishers, Incorporated for "The Busy Farmer's Wife," "The Shopping Trip," "The Lion Hunt," and "One Finger Keep Moving" from *Fun and Games* by Margaret

Index of Titles